The Pink Tornado

Subtopic: *Tongue on Display*

James A. Durr

The Pink Tornado

Subtopic: Tongue on Display

Unless otherwise indicated all Scripture quotations are taken from the King James Version of the Bible.

The Pink Tornado
"Tongue on Display"

James A. Durr
965 Morton Road
Anniston, Alabama 36205
jamesdurr3@yahoo.com

Printed in the United States of America

Published by: James A. Durr
965 Morton Road
Anniston, Alabama 36205

Edited by: Benita Duff /James Durr
Cover Layout and Design by: James Durr/D.J. Hall (17) & Benita Duff.
Photography: Benita Duff/ Blessed Wind Media Group
Anniston, Alabama 36201

Table of Contents

*Death and life are in **the power of the tongue:** and **they that love it shall eat the fruit** thereof.*

Proverbs 18:21

Acknowledgement

- I give all glory and honor to Yahuah (My Heavenly Father), Yahusha (My Adonai and Redeemer) and the precious Ruach HaKodesh (My best friend).
- To my wonderful wife, Dr. Kim (I love you dearly girlfriend) and I pray that Elohyim richly bless your music ministry.
- To my children Kalina, Lisa, DJ (thanks for the drawings), DeJuan and Jasmine (I am so grateful that Elohyim placed you guys in my life). I love you all!
- To the saints at The Word Center International (TWCI). Thanks for not giving up on me! "Let's do this!" I Love You!
- To my Mother Katherine A. Williams, love you! Too my Father James L. Durr and his lovely wife Venus love you both! To all my brothers and sisters natural and spiritual - I love you all!
- To Apostle Ernest and Apostle Emma Dickens Love You Both and The Kingdom Empowerment Ministry (K.E.M.)
- To Apostle and Pastor Horton love you both (7000) more!
- To The (Late) Apostle Gary and Apostle Phyllis Morton & SRCC love you!
- To Pastor Christine Robinson and Asst Pastor Chris Hardy and Hope Over comer Ministries. Bless you all!
- To Apostle/Dr. Andra Cunningham and Dr. Lady Cunningham & NLCC Go for It!
- Apostle Dr. Maurice K. Wright/Lady Wright & UCC- Thank you also for the Haverim fellowship!
- To all of Elohyim's people that love me in-spite of me. I love you back, with the love of HaMashiach!

My desire is to speak with: compassion, conviction, confidence and be convincing to the hearts, the minds and souls of men all over this world.

James Anthony Durr

Introduction:

I remember how this book came together. I was outside on my porch getting ready to finish reading a book. The book was entitled: **Redeemed Talk by: Apostle Halton "Skip" Horton.** Before, I got to it; Yahuah began to speak to me about an outline I had in my I-Phone of a book I had just completed. Yah wanted me to erase all of the information out of my phone and I responded with "Father that is a lot of information" and his reply was erase it; you have the book and the information on your hard drive. So I complied! Not long after that Elohyim, began to drop information on me about a message I had taught some 18 years ago. **Entitled: Beware of the Pink Tornado!** As the revelation of the message kept coming I took out my I-Phone and began to type and therefore you have it; this very book. I am so grateful to EL for this assignment and I believe that you will be blessed by the insight and wisdom you will gain.

"Walking in the Supernatural"

James A. Durr

The Pink Tornado

Chapter 1

The Pink Tornado!
Subtopic: Tongue on Display

Let the words of my mouth, and the meditation of my heart, be acceptable in thy sight, O YAHUAH, my strength, and my redeemer.   ***Psalm 19:14***

Wherefore I say unto you, All manner of sin and blasphemy shall be forgiven unto men: but the blasphemy against the Ruach HaKodesh shall not be forgiven unto men. ***And whosoever speaketh a word against the Son of man, it shall be forgiven him: but whosoever speaketh against the Ruach HaKodesh, it shall not be forgiven him, neither in this world, neither in the world to come.*** *Either make the tree good, and his fruit good; or else make the tree corrupt, and his fruit corrupt: for the tree is known by his fruit. O generation of vipers,* ***how can ye, being evil, speak good things? For out of the abundance of the heart the mouth speaketh.*** *A good man out of the good treasure of the heart bringeth forth good things: and an evil man out of the evil treasure bringeth forth evil things.* ***But I say unto you, that every idle word that men shall speak, they shall give account thereof in the Day of Judgment.***

For by thy words thou shalt be justified, and by thy words thou shalt be condemned.   *Matthew 1:31-37*

Definition:

Word: A unit of language that native speakers can identify.
> *A verbal command for action*
> *An exchange of views on some topic*

Tongue: A human written or spoken language used by a
> *Community.*
> *A manner of speaking.*

Tornado: A localized and violently destructive windstorm
> *occurring over land characterized by a funnel-shaped cloud extending towards the ground.*

The reason I have I entitled this book: The Pink Tornado is because; over the years I have seen the damage this small body part can produce. *The word tornado fits the tongue perfectly because, of its potential to be used to speak good and yet be a destructive force at the same time.*

When a tornado hits the ground; it hits the ground running and if you're in its path, you will get hit. It shows no remorse, no sympathy, and apologizes to no one. That's the way most people are today; they stir up mess, they backbite, lie, and they gossip! A tornado reminds me of a selfish person (me, me, and me): It could care less about what and how others are feeling; it just wants its way. Just look at the end results of every strong tornado; lives are lost, debris is left behind, people lose valuable items and now recovery has to be set in motion. This is all because of **one event** occurring! *The same goes for the tongue; it only needs **one opportunity** to damage someone else's life; if given the chance. <u>With our tongue we can curse you out and turn right around and bless you within the next hour. The tongue is the only one that can get you and me into some great places and into some dark places. The tongue the bible states can no man tame.</u>* Why? Because, it only speaks what it's been exposed to. So we must keep our tongue in check! And in order for us as Believers to keep our mouth in check we must stay prayed up, and studied up in Elohyim's word.

*-The Bible is the infallible **Word of EL***
*-**Yahusha is the Word** made flesh*
*-**The Ruach Hakodesh illuminates the Word of EL** and brings clarity to our situation.*

Set a watch, O Yahuah, before my mouth; keep the door of my lips.   **Psalm 141:3**

Teach us how to speak O YAH, according to thy Word!

We must understand that EL is not only bound to his word in the Holy Bible itself but, unto every word that proceeds from his mouth. If he says it: It has to be done. The same goes for us. He does not want us to speak so hastily and not make good on what we have spoken. The reason The Most High Yahuah is pushing us to do the same is because we are his representatives in the earth and we must operate in the same manner he does. All I am saying to you is that if El has ever spoken anything to you, its money in the bank. The check won't bounce! He will make good on his promise.

Keep thy foot when thou goest to the house of Elohyim, **and be more ready to hear, than to give the sacrifice of fools**: *For they consider not that they do evil.* **Be not rash with thy mouth,** *and let not thine heart* **be hasty to utter anything** *before EL: For Elohyim is in heaven, and thou upon earth:* **Therefore let thy words be few.** *For a dream cometh through the multitude of business; and a* **fool's voice is known by multitude of words.**

When thou vowest a vow unto EL, defer not to pay it; for he hath no pleasure in fools: pay that which thou hast vowed. Better is it that thou shouldest not vow, than that thou shouldest vow and not pay. Suffer not thy mouth to cause thy flesh to sin; neither say thou before the angel, that it was an error: *wherefore should EL be angry at thy voice, and destroy the work of thine hands? For in the multitude of dreams and many words* there are also divers vanities: *but fear thou Elohyim.*

Ecclesiastes 5:1-7

*Wherefore, my beloved brethren, **let every man be swift to hear, slow to speak, slow to wrath:***

James 1:19

- *The Tongue can be a force for good or a force for evil*

- *Beware if the tongue is used for evil; it could bring about devastating consequences.*

- *But, if it is used for good; it could wreak havoc on the forces of evil and bless everyone and everything else that's involved with the success of Yahuah's Kingdom.*

14

My brethren, be not many masters, knowing that we shall receive the greater condemnation. **For in many things we offend all. If any man offend not in word, the same is a perfect man, and able also to bridle the whole body.** *Behold, we put bits in the horses' mouths, that they may obey us; and we turn about their whole body. Behold also the ships, which though they be so great, and are driven of fierce winds, yet are they turned about with a very small helm, whithersoever the governor listeth.* **Even so the tongue is a little member, and boasteth great things. Behold how great a matter a little fire kindleth! And the tongue is a fire, a world of iniquity: so is the tongue among our members, that it defileth the whole body, and setteth on fire the course of nature; and it is set on fire of hell.** *For every kind of beasts, and of birds, and of serpents, and of things in the sea, is tamed, and hath been tamed of mankind:* **But the tongue can no man tame; it is an unruly evil, full of deadly poison. Therewith bless we Elohyim, even the Father; and therewith curse we men, which are made after the similitude of Elohyim. Out of the same mouth proceedeth blessing and cursing. My brethren, these things ought not so to be. Doth a fountain send forth at the same place sweet water and bitter? Can the fig tree, my brethren, bear olive berries? Either a vine, figs? so can no fountain both yield salt water and fresh.** *Who is a wise man and endued with knowledge among you? Let him show out of a good conversation his works with meekness of wisdom.* ***James 3:1-13***

In James chapter three (3) which is considered the ultimate chapter on the tongue. You can see for yourself how self-explanatory it is when it comes to the operation and dynamics of the tongue. We must take our time and study this section over and over again until we have the full revelation on this subject. Now, let me ask you a question. Are you sure you want the task of changing the way you speak? If you do: You must stop the use of empty words and fruitless talk. For if you change it; it will definitely change you and the way you see things, do things and with whom you associate with? Don't just be in the crowd; talking loud and saying nothing!

When it comes to change refer to these two passages of scripture:

And he spake also a parable unto them; No man putteth a piece of a new garment upon an old; if otherwise, then both the new maketh a rent, and the piece that was taken out of the new agreeth not with the old. ***And no man putteth new wine into old bottles; else the new wine will burst the bottles, and be spilled, and the bottles shall perish. But new wine must be put into new bottles; and both are preserved.*** *No man also having drunk old wine straightway desireth new: for he saith, the old is better.*

Luke 5:37-39

*And herein I give my advice: for this is expedient for you, who have begun before, **not only to do, but also to be forward a year ago. Now therefore perform the doing of it; that as there was a readiness to will, so there may be a performance also out of that which ye have. For if there be first a willing mind, it is accepted according to that a man hath, and not according to that he hath not.** For I mean not that other men be eased, and ye burdened:* **II Corinthians 8:10-13**

We have to understand we can't just say anything we want and think that there is no consequence for our actions; for our words are conveying messages to either build up or to tear down.

People say things like:

- *He had us laughing to death! "Oh really?"*
- *You make me sick! "You will get what you say!"*
- *That situation is worrying me to death!*
- *Man, I almost had a heart attack laughing so hard!*
- *Man, when I saw that roller coaster size, I all most passed out.*
- *Girl! You are a hot mess. "What!"*
- *You are so silly! (look up the word)*

*I call this <u>**Death Talk 101**</u>! If you keep speaking it; you will eventually eat the fruit of it.*

YAH never opens his mouth by mistake; it's always on purpose.

*My son, if thou be surety for thy friend, if thou hast stricken thy hand with a stranger, **Thou art snared with the words of thy mouth, thou art taken with the words of thy mouth.**   Proverbs 6:1-2*

*The lips of the righteous know what is acceptable: but the **mouth of the wicked speaketh frowardness.***
Proverbs 10:32

*By the blessing of the upright the city is exalted: **but it is overthrown by the mouth of the wicked.** Proverbs 11:11*

***Only let your conversation be as it becometh the gospel of HaMashiach: that whether I come and see you, or else be absent**, I may hear of your affairs, that ye stand fast in one spirit, with one mind striving together for the faith of the gospel;*
Philippians 1:27

In Apostle "Skip" Horton Book: Redeemed Talk: "Let the Redeemed of Yahuah say so!"

Apostle Horton wrote a profound statement and it stuck with me; He said in the forward section page 3 of the book*: It's not what you say, it's what you keep saying, this is what will be remembered*

- *So people will remember you not just for what you do; but, also for what you say.*
- *So we can cause problems by what we say or do not say!*

*If it's
not
coming
out of Elohyim's
mouth;
it shouldn't be
coming out of
your mouth.*

The Enemy Knows

Chapter 2

The Enemy Knows!
Genesis 3:1-7

Now the serpent was more subtle than any beast of the field which Yahuah Elohyim had made. ***And he said unto the woman,*** Yea, hath EL said, ye shall not eat of every tree of the garden? ***And the woman said*** unto the serpent, we may eat of the fruit of the trees of the garden: But of the fruit of the tree which *is* in the midst of the garden, EL hath said, ye shall not eat of it, neither shall ye touch it, lest ye die. ***And the serpent said unto the woman, ye shall not surely die: For EL doth know that in the day ye eat thereof, then your eyes shall be opened, and ye shall be as gods, knowing good and evil.*** *And when the woman saw* that the tree *was* good for food, and that it *was* pleasant to the eyes, and a tree to be desired to make *one* wise*, she took of the fruit thereof, and did eat, and gave also unto her husband with her; and he did eat.* And the eyes of them both were opened, and they knew that they *were* naked; and they sewed fig leaves together, and made themselves aprons.

Genesis 3:-17

Look at this verse:

*Death and life are in the power of the tongue: and **they that love it shall eat the fruit thereof.*** *Proverbs 18:21*

This information I'm about to relay to you is very important and vital to the Body of Messiah. We need to know the Word of YAH and when he his speaking to us; because, Satan is standing there ready to twist the message you and I are about to receive that will help us fulfill our destiny in Messiah. *Our enemy knows the power of the spoken word!* This is the reason he chose **to speak** to Eve and not just do animal tricks through the serpent. I believe Satan knew if he showed up in spirit form in the earth realm he would be operating illegally in the earth without a body; for this is a law of EL; *(this is why EL prepared Yahusha a body to come and redeem the world).* So after Satan occupied the body of the serpent to perform his assignment; he was able to show up in front of Eve. *I believe after much study of the couple's daily routine and activities; he finally figured out what he had to do. I can imagine in my sanctified mind that he said I'll just be nice and talk with her to see if she will take a bite of my words; along with her husband, who was with her (close proximity). As we know: Adam had the power to subdue anything that got out of line but, did nothing and we are paying for this one mistake of* **when he should have spoken up and didn't.**

Beware of deceitful lips.

Remember:
*He also tried to **use this strategy of words** with EL about his servant Job.*   ***Job 2:1-10***

He spoke** to rebellious angels in Heaven in an attempt to overthrow Yahuah off of his throne **(you know the outcome).

***The Explanation of Lucifer's fall:** All bark and no real bite when it comes to EL*

*Moreover the word of Yahuah came unto me, saying, Son of man, take up a lamentation upon the king of Tyrus, and say unto him, Thus saith Yahuah Elohyim; Thou sealest up the sum, full of wisdom, and perfect in beauty. **Thou hast been in Eden the garden of EL;** every precious stone was thy covering, the sardius, topaz, and the diamond, the beryl, the onyx, and the jasper, the sapphire, the emerald, and the carbuncle, and gold: the workmanship of thy tabrets and of thy pipes was prepared in thee in the day that thou wast created. **Thou art the anointed cherub that covereth; and I have set thee so: thou wast upon the holy mountain of EL; thou hast walked up and down in the midst of the stones of fire.***

*Thou wast perfect in thy ways from the day that thou wast created, till iniquity was found in thee. By the multitude of thy merchandise they have filled the midst of thee with violence, and thou hast sinned: therefore I will cast thee as profane out of the mountain of EL: and I will destroy thee, O covering cherub, from the midst of the stones of fire. **Thine heart was lifted up because of thy beauty; thou hast corrupted thy wisdom by reason of thy brightness: I will cast thee to the ground; I will lay thee before kings, that they may behold thee. Thou hast defiled thy sanctuaries by the multitude of thine iniquities, by the iniquity of thy traffic; therefore will I bring forth a fire from the midst of thee, it shall devour thee**, and I will bring thee to ashes upon the earth in the sight of all them that behold thee. All they that know thee among the people shall be astonished at thee: thou shalt be a terror, and never shalt thou be any more.*

Ezekiel 28:11-19

Another reference from the Word of Elohyim:

Hell from beneath is moved for thee to meet thee at thy coming: it stirreth up the dead for thee, even all the chief ones of the earth; it hath raised up from their thrones all the kings of the nations. All they shall speak and say unto thee, Art thou also become weak as we?

Art thou become like unto us? Thy pomp is brought down to the grave, and the noise of thy viols: the worm is spread under thee, and the worms cover thee. How art thou fallen from heaven, **O Lucifer, son of the morning! How art thou cut down to the ground, which didst weaken the nations! For thou hast said in thine heart, I will ascend into heaven, I will exalt my throne above the stars of Elohyim: I will sit also upon the mount of the congregation, in the sides of the north: I will ascend above the heights of the clouds; I will be like the most High. Yet thou shalt be brought down to hell, to the sides of the pit. They that see thee shall narrowly look upon thee, and consider thee, saying, is this the man that made the earth to tremble, that did shake kingdoms;** *That made the world as a wilderness, and destroyed the cities thereof; that opened not the house of his prisoners? All the kings of the nations, even all of them, lie in glory, everyone in his own house. But thou art cast out of thy grave like an abominable branch, and as the raiment of those that are slain, thrust through with a sword, that go down to the stones of the pit; as a carcase trodden under feet. Thou shalt not be joined with them in burial, because thou hast destroyed thy land, and slain thy people: the seed of evildoers shall never be renowned.*

Isaiah 14:9-20

Look at the outcome of Lucifer! His words got him in trouble! Even if he (Satan) or his associates come up against you; here is a scripture remedy for this situation:

No weapon that is formed against thee shall prosper; and every tongue *that shall rise against thee in judgment thou shalt condemn. This is the heritage of the servants of Yahuah, and their righteousness is of me, saith Yahuah.*   ***Isaiah 54:17***

He also came up against Yahusha **with words** *in the wilderness during his hour of temptation.* ***Matthew 4:4***

But, I love the way Yahusha responded to the enemy. He not only spoke back to him with words but, with the Word of EL. For Yahusha is the Word made flesh and that dwelled among us. So Satan was really trying to use Elohyim's word with a twist to twist the Word himself (Yahusha).

It didn't work!

Word Power

Speak the Word Only

Chapter 3

Speak the Word Only!
Matthew 8:5:13

And when Yahusha was entered into Capernaum, **there came unto him a centurion***, beseeching him, and saying,* **Adonai, my servant lieth at home sick of the palsy, grievously tormented. And Yahusha saith unto him, I will come and heal him.** *The centurion answered and said, Adonai, I am not worthy that thou shouldest come under my roof:* **but speak the word only, and my servant shall be healed.** *For I am a man under authority, having soldiers under me: and I say to this man, Go, and he goeth; and to another, Come, and he cometh; and to my servant, Do this, and he doeth it.* **When Yahusha heard it, he marvelled, and said to them that followed, Verily I say unto you, I have not found so great faith, no, not in Yashar'el.** *And I say unto you, that many shall come from the east and west, and shall sit down with Abraham, and Isaac, and Jacob, in the kingdom of Yahusha. But the children of the kingdom shall be cast out into outer darkness: There shall be weeping and gnashing of teeth.* **And Yahusha said unto the centurion, Go thy way; and as thou hast believed, so be it done unto thee. And his servant was healed in the selfsame hour.**

Matthew 8:5-13

30

What a faith filled conversation between Yahusha and the Centurion soldier; who knew the power of EL by observation. He knew all Adonai had to do was **SPEAK THE WORD** only and his servant would be healed. Today, in most religious settings if the preacher said I am coming over; we expect him to show up. But, if he says I'll speak a word of prayer over your loved one and Elohyim is going to heal them because, I can't make it by your house today, before he finished speaking they would have changed and cut them off. Unless they are mature enough to handle the leader's instructions.

The Syrophenician or Canaanite woman: *Another example of words filled with faith.*

Then Yahusha went thence, and departed into the coasts of Tyre and Sidon. ***And, behold, a woman of Canaan came out of the same coasts, and cried unto him, saying, Have mercy on me, O Adonai, thou Son of David; my daughter is grievously vexed with a devil.*** *But he answered her not a word. And his disciples came and besought him, saying, send her away; for she crieth after us. But he answered and said, I am not sent but unto the lost sheep of the house of Israel.* ***Then came she and worshipped him, saying, Adonai, help me. But he answered and said, It is not meet to take the children's bread, and to cast it to dogs.*** *And she said, Truth, Lord: yet the dogs eat of the crumbs which fall from their masters' table.*

31

Then Adonai answered and said unto her, O woman, great is thy faith: be it unto thee even as thou wilt. And her daughter was made whole from that very hour.

The mouth of a righteous man is a well of life: but violence covereth the mouth of the wicked.
Proverbs 10:11

*The tongue of the just is as choice silver: the heart of the wicked is little worth. **The lips of the righteous feed many:** but fools die for want of wisdom.*
Proverbs 10:20-21

There is that speaketh like the piercings of a sword: **but the tongue of the wise is health. The lip of truth shall be established for ever:** *but a lying tongue is but for a moment.* **Proverbs 12:18-19**

Whoso keepeth his mouth and his tongue keepeth his soul from troubles. **Proverbs 21:23**

- ✦ *Yahusha spoke everything into existence (Colossians 1)*
- ✦ *Yahusha cursed the fig tree for faking production (Mark 11)*

+ *Yahusha spoke and Lazarus came out of the grave (John 11)*
+ *Elijah called down fire from Heaven and it consumed all that was in the way. (I Kings 18)*

*Here is a perfect example of not speaking what **Yahuah** says to speak:*

Moses is a prime example of when Yahuah says to speak his word; his word should be spoken. Never let your desires or frustration; make you miss out on EL's best. Moses did not sanctify Elohyim before the people and it cost him a trip to the Promised Land.

So we must take Elohyim at his word and speak His word on a daily basis.

<u>Encouragement</u>

EL

Is

In

Love

With

You!

Words
Are
Powerful

Chapter 4

Words are Powerful!
Proverbs 15:4/Proverbs 17:4

A wholesome tongue is a tree of life: but perverseness
therein is a breach in the spirit.   ***Proverbs 15:4***

A wicked doer giveth heed to false lips; and a liar
giveth ear to a naughty tongue.   ***Proverbs 17:4***

Excellent speech becometh not a fool: much less do
lying lips a prince.   ***Proverbs 17:7***

I wrote a song entitled: ***Word Power*** *and it was taken*
from the scripture:

For the word of Elohyim is quick, and powerful, and
sharper than any twoedged sword, *piercing even to the*
dividing asunder of soul and spirit, and of the joints and
marrow, and is a discerner of the thoughts and intents of
the heart.   ***Hebrew 4:12***

Look at the power of the spoken word spoken to Peter's
ruach which caused him to walk on the water.

+ Peter *on the command of Yahusha* walked on water and once he took his eyes off Adonai he almost drowned; but he was saved from drowning **with a word.** (Peter & Yahusha)

+ The Syrophenician woman whose daughter was grievously vexed with a Devil and *she spoke to Yahusha and said to him after he called her a dog; even the dog eat the crumbs that fall from the masters table.* (The Syrophenician Woman & Yahusha)

Remember the saying: Sticks and stones my brake my bones but, words will never hurt me.

My response: That's a Lie!

+ The enemy spoke to Cain's mind and he slew his brother (Abel) because, he knew that Abel had offered up to EL a better sacrifice than his. But, *Abel's blood began to speak from the ground up to EL.* And Elohyim responded to it. (Cain & Abel)

+ Words have gotten more people killed than any other methods: (David & Uriah)

+ Elijah also heard what Queen Jezebel *said she* was going to do to him, and *her words* became a picturesque view in his mind and he ran and hid in a cave. (Elijah & Queen Jezebel).

- Words are the cause of many relationships going bad. (David & Ahitophel). This is Bathsheba's Grandfather who wanted revenge on David for what he did to her).

- Words have caused many to become emotionally unstable or suicidal. (Judas and the Priest) also (David and Ahitophel) both betrayers hung themselves.

Speak it into Existence

Chapter 5

Speak it into Existence!
Genesis 1

In the beginning Elohyim created the heaven and the earth. *And the earth was without form, and void; and darkness was upon the face of the deep.* ***And the Ruach of EL moved upon*** *the face of the waters.* ***And EL said, Let there be light: and there was light.*** *And EL saw the light, that it was good: and EL divided the light from the darkness. And EL called the light Day, and the darkness he called Night. And the evening and the morning were the first day.* ***Genesis 1:1-5***

For by him were all things created, that are in heaven, and that are in earth, visible and invisible, whether they be thrones, or dominions, or principalities, or powers: all things were created by him, and for him: *And he is before all things, and by him all things consist.*

Colossians 1:16-17

*When EL created things that exist in the earth **he did it with his mouth.** So when he **spoke it; it** became what he said it would be. What a remarkable way of getting what you want done and you don't have to lift a finger.*

But, when it came to mankind he not only spoke but, **EL said he was going to make man** *in his image and in his likeness* **so he put his hands on him and breathed into him.**

Here are a few Hebrew words to explain God EL's creative process of man.

Hebrew: Yatsar *(3335) meaning; to form (he touched man) hands on, framed him:*

- *The Potter's Touch*
- *To fashion*
- *To make*

Hebrew:

 Naphach *(5301) meaning; to breathe or blow. Yah breathed himself into man.*
Neshamah *(5395 meaning; to breathe, spirit of, blast into and inspiration.*

When Elohyim put the finishing touches on Adam; he blew his creative abilities into him and he became a living soul. *Now EL did all of this by design so Adam* **could do as he did and speak as he spoke into things.**

Look at EL!

Now faith is the substance of things hoped for, the evidence of things not seen. For by it the elders obtained a good report. **Through faith we understand that the worlds were framed by the word of EL,** *so that things which are seen were not made of things which do appear.*   **Hebrew11:1-3**

Elohyim used faith filled words to create snap shots of each world and framed them by his word. What a mighty EL we serve!

If we are made in the image and likeliness of our Heavenly Father which is in heaven; **then we can do as our Father has done call those things which be not as though they were.** We must not limit ourselves; we need to be stretching out on faith and releasing faith filled words into the atmosphere. Faith unleashed is like a hound dog on the trail of a scent of something it is seeking after. **Seek him faith!**

The preparations of the heart in man, and **the answer of the tongue, is from Yahuah.**
                    Proverbs 16:1

Adam followed suit:

*And out of the ground Yahuah Elohyim formed every beast of the field, and every fowl of the air; **and brought them unto <u>Adam</u> <u>to see what he would call</u> <u>them: and whatsoever Adam called every living creature,</u> <u>that was the name thereof.</u> <u>And Adam gave names to all</u> <u>cattle, and to the fowl of the air, and to every beast of the</u> <u>field</u>**; but for Adam there was not found an help meet for him.*

Genesis 2:19-20

    ⬥ We need to be doing the same, the Father is
        not pleased if we don't.
    ⬥ EL said that the just shall live by faith.

For we walk by faith, not by sight   **II Corinthians 5:7**

Even in our salvation we had to talk. *For if we hadn't talked our salvation wouldn't have manifested**: It says with the mouth confession is made unto salvation!***

    *But what saith it? <u>The word is nigh thee, even in thy</u> <u>mouth, and in thy heart:</u> that is, the word of faith, which we preach; <u>That if thou shalt confess with thy mouth the</u> <u>Adonai Yahusha,</u> and shalt believe in thine heart that EL hath raised him from the dead, thou shalt be saved. For with the heart man believeth unto righteousness; **<u>and</u>** **<u>with the mouth confession is made unto salvation.</u>***

For the scripture saith, whosoever believeth on him shall not be ashamed. For there is no difference between the Jew and the Greek: for the same Adonai over all is rich unto all that call upon him. <u>For whosoever shall call upon the name of Adonai shall be saved.</u> How then shall they call on him in whom they have not believed? And how shall they believe in him of whom they have not heard? And how shall they hear without a preacher? And how shall they preach, except they be sent? As it is written, how beautiful are the feet of them that preach the gospel of peace, and bring glad tidings of good things! But they have not all obeyed the gospel. For Esaias saith, Yahuah, who hath believed our report? **So then faith cometh by hearing, and hearing by the word of Yahuah.** *But I say, have they not heard? Yes verily, their sound went into all the earth, and their words unto the ends of the world.* ***Romans 10:8-18***

Let us hold fast the profession of our faith without wavering; (for he is faithful that promised): *And let us consider one another to provoke unto love and to good works: Not forsaking the assembling of ourselves together, as the manner of some is; but exhorting one another: and so much the more, as ye see the day approaching.* ***Hebrew 10:23-25***

Cast not away therefore your confidence, which hath great recompense of reward. For ye have need of patience, that, after ye have done the will of Yahuah, ye might receive the promise. *For yet a little while, and he that shall come will come, and will not tarry. Now the just shall live by faith: but if any man draws back, my soul shall have no pleasure in him.* But we are not of them who draw back unto perdition; but of them that believe to the saving of the soul.   *Hebrews 10:35-39*

Abraham believed and spoke what EL said and just look at the end results. Now we are partakers and called the seed of Abraham. The bible also says that the blessings of Abraham are upon us. Because, of one man's mouth speaking what EL spoke we are blessed forever.

*For the promise, that he should be the heir of the world, was not to Abraham, or to his seed, through the law, **but through the righteousness of faith.** For if they which are of the law be heirs, faith is made void, and the promise made of none effect: Because the law worketh wrath: for where no law is, there is no transgression*

Therefore it is of faith, that it might be by grace; to the end the promise might be sure to all the seed; not to that only which is of the law, but to that also which is of the faith of Abraham; who is the father of us all, (As it is written, I have made thee a father of many nations,) before him whom he believed, even EL, who quickeneth the dead, and calleth those things which be not as though they were. Who against hope believed in hope, that he might become the father of many nations, according to that which was spoken, so shall thy seed be. And being not weak in faith, he considered not his own body now dead, when he was about an hundred years old, neither yet the deadness of Sarah's womb: He staggered not at the promise of EL through unbelief; but was strong in faith, giving glory to EL; And being fully persuaded that, what he had promised, he was able also **to perform.** And therefore it was imputed to him for righteousness. **Romans 4:13-22**

Remember: Elohyim is committed to performing his word:

Then said Yahuah unto me, *Thou hast well seen:* **for I will hasten my word to perform it. Jeremiah 1:12**

46

You may be saying preacher: I am having a hard time believing EL. For there are some things I prayed for a long time ago and they had yet to come to pass? What should I do? *I'll tell you that it won't happen without faith and works together; you can forget that.* You have to put your faith back to work and start talking about the things you desire to see Elohyim do for you.

What doth it profit, my brethren, though a man say he hath faith, and have not works? Can faith save him? If a brother or sister be naked, and destitute of daily food, And one of you say unto them, Depart in peace, be ye warmed and filled; notwithstanding ye give them not those things which are needful to the body; what doth it profit? Even so faith, if it hath not works, is dead, being alone. Yea, a man may say, Thou hast faith, and I have works: show me thy faith without thy works, and I will show thee my faith by my works. Thou believest that there is one EL; thou doest well: the devils also believe, and tremble. But wilt thou know, O vain man, that faith without works is dead? Was not Abraham our father justified by works, when he had offered Isaac his son upon the altar? Seest thou how faith wrought with his works and by works was faith made perfect? And the scripture was fulfilled which saith, Abraham believed EL, and it was imputed unto him for righteousness: and he was called the Friend of Elohyim.

Ye see then how that by works a man is justified, and not by faith only. Likewise also was not Rahab the harlot justified by works, when she had received the messengers, and had sent them out another way? For as the body without the spirit is dead, so faith without works is dead also.   ***James 2:17-26***

Look at Daniel's situation; when he prayed and his prayers were hindered by the Prince of Persia (the demonic influence over that area). But, the answer from Elohyim was on the way the first day that Daniel prayed to Elohyim. The angel of EL finally broke through and came into Daniel room and spoke to him:

And he said unto me, ***O Daniel, a man greatly beloved, understand the words that I speak unto thee, and stand upright:*** *for unto thee am I now sent.* ***And when he had spoken this word unto me,*** *I stood trembling. Then said he unto me,* <u>*Fear not, Daniel*</u>*:* <u>***for from the first day that thou didst set thine heart to understand, and to chasten thyself***</u> *before thy Elohyim,* <u>***thy words were heard, and I am come for thy words.***</u> *But the prince of the kingdom of Persia withstood me one and twenty days: but, lo, Michael, one of the chief princes, came to help me; and I remained there with the kings of Persia.*   ***Daniel 10:11-13***

Look at what the angel came for: **Daniels words.** This is why we need to be saying something when we feel the unction of EL to pray or to say anything.

Learn how to talk yourself out of it:

And Yahusha answering saith unto them, Have faith in Yahuah. **For verily I say unto you, That whosoever shall say unto this mountain, Be thou removed, and be thou cast into the sea; and shall not doubt in his heart, but shall believe that those things which he saith shall come to pass; he shall have whatsoever he saith.** *Therefore I say unto you, what things so ever ye desire, when ye pray, believe that ye receive them, and ye shall have them.*   ***Mark 11:22-24***

And Balaam said unto Balak, Lo, I am come unto thee: have I now any power **at all to say anything? The word that EL putteth in my mouth, that shall I speak.**   ***Numbers 22:38***

Then Yahuah put forth his hand, and touched my mouth. **And Yahuah said unto me, Behold, I have put my words in thy mouth.**   ***Jeremiah 1:9***

And they overcame him by the blood of the Lamb, and **by the word of their testimony;** *and they loved not their lives unto the death.*   ***Revelation 12:11***

For Yahuah giveth wisdom: **Out of his mouth cometh knowledge and understanding.** *He layeth up sound wisdom for the righteous: he is a buckler to them that walk uprightly.*

Proverbs 2:6

Get wisdom, get understanding: forget it not; **neither decline from the words of my mouth.**   **Proverbs 4:5**

But he answered and said, it is written, Man shall not live by bread alone, **but by every word that proceedeth out of the mouth of EL.**   **Matthew 4:4**

It
Shall
Come
To
Pass

Chapter 6

It shall come to Pass
Numbers 23:18-26

And he took up his parable, and said, Rise up, Balak, and hear; hearken unto me, thou son of Zippor: **Elohyim is not a man, that he should lie; neither the son of man, that he should repent: hath he said, and shall he not do it? Or hath he spoken, and shall he not make it good? Behold, I have received commandment to bless: and he hath blessed; and I cannot reverse it.** *He hath not beheld iniquity in Jacob, neither hath he seen perverseness in Israel: Yahuah his Elohyim is with him, and the shout of a king is among them. EL brought them out of Egypt; he hath as it were the strength of an unicorn. Surely there is no enchantment against Jacob, neither is there any divination against Yashar'el: according to this time it shall be said of Jacob and of Yashar'el, What hath EL wrought! Behold, the people shall rise up as a great lion, and lift up himself as a young lion: he shall not lie down until he eat of the prey, and drink the blood of the slain.* **And Balak said unto Balaam,** *Neither curse them at all, nor bless them at all.* **But Balaam answered and said unto Balak, Told not I thee, saying, All that the Yahuah speaketh, that I must do?**
Numbers 23:18-26

*Then shalt thou delight thyself in Yahuah; and I will cause thee to ride upon the high places of the earth, and feed thee with the heritage of Jacob thy father: **for the mouth of Yahuah hath spoken it.***   ***Isaiah 58:14***

For all the promises of EL in him are yea, and in him Amen, *unto the glory of EL by us.* ***II Corinthians 1:20***

Neither have I gone back from the commandment of his lips; ***I have esteemed the words of his mouth*** *more than my necessary food.*   ***Job 23:12***

+ *Elohyim is a fulfiller of purposes*
+ *Elohyim is a Giver of Dreams*
+ *We are the Dream Liver's*

Elohyim is a keeper of his promises! If it comes out of his mouth he has to perform it. EL is bonded to his words.

For verily I say unto you, till heaven and earth pass, one jot or one tittle shall in no wise pass from the law, till all be fulfilled.   **Matthew 5:18**

And it is easier for heaven and earth to pass, than one tittle of the law to fail.   **Luke 16:17**

   I am so glad that *Elohyim is a covenant keeper; that if he makes a promise to you before you die he is able to perform it. I have witness many of the words that EL spoke over my life come to pass and many others will eventually come to pass when the set time has occurred and everything is in place for all to transpire.*

Elohyim is yet keeping his word!

- He made a covenant with Abraham
- He gave Joseph a dream
- He made Hanna a promise
- He made a covenant with King David
- He extended King Hezekiah's life
- He made a promise to save all Israel
- He made a promise to you and I to save our whole household

He that keepeth Yashar'el never sleeps nor slumbers:

So if EL said it; he's big enough, awesome enough and great enough to bring it to pass.

Want he do it!

Elohyim is not a man, that he should lie; neither the son of man, that he should repent: hath he said, and shall he not do it? Or hath he spoken, and shall he not make it good?

54

*Behold, I have received commandment to bless:
and he hath blessed; and I cannot reverse it.*
                              Numbers 23:19-20

*For my thoughts are not your thoughts, neither are your
ways my ways, saith Yahuah For as the heavens are
higher than the earth, so are my ways higher than your
ways, and my thoughts than your thoughts. For as the
rain cometh down, and the snow from heaven, and
returneth not thither, but watereth the earth, and maketh
it bring forth and bud, that it may give seed to the sower,
and bread to the eater:* ***So shall my word be that goeth
forth out of my mouth: it shall not return unto me void,
but it shall accomplish that which I please, and it shall
prosper in the thing whereto I sent it. For ye shall go
out with joy, and be led forth with peace: the
mountains and the hills shall break forth before you
into singing, and all the trees of the field shall
clap their hands.*** *Instead of the thorn shall come up the
fir tree, and instead of the brier shall come up the myrtle
tree: and it shall be to Yahuah for a name, for an
everlasting sign that shall not be cut off.*
                              Isaiah 55:8-13

So don't worry, don't give in do your best to keep the
faith in what The Most High Yahuah has spoken to you.
And even if you feel lonely, discouraged and can't see
no way out; you can depend on Yah to do what he said.
For He will give you and I strength to complete the
journey ahead.

Hast thou not known? Hast thou not heard that the everlasting Elohyim, Yahuah, the Creator of the ends of the earth, fainteth not, neither is weary? There is no searching of his understanding. **He giveth power to the faint; and to them that have no might he increaseth strength.** *Even the youths shall faint and be weary, and the young men shall utterly fall:* **But they that wait upon Yahuah shall renew their strength; they shall mount up with wings as eagles; they shall run, and not be weary; and they shall walk, and not faint.**

Isaiah 40:28-31

Yahuah, give us the strength to wait it out!

I will stand upon my watch, and set me upon the tower, and will watch to see what he will say unto me, and what I shall answer when I am reproved. **And Yahuah answered me, and said**, *write the vision, and make it plain upon tables, that he may run that readeth it.* **For the vision is yet for an appointed time, but at the end it shall speak, and not lie: though it tarry, wait for it; because it will surely come, it will not tarry.** *Behold, his soul which is lifted up is not upright in him: but the just shall live by his faith.*   **Habakkuk 2:1-4**

Man those are two very powerful passages of scripture!

They will keep us victorious, encouraged and speaking by faith until we see the manifestation of every miracle the Most High Yahuah has in store for us.

56

And the word of Yahuah came unto me, saying, Son of
man, what is that proverb that ye have in the land of
Yahsar'el, saying, *the days are prolonged, and every
vision faileth? Tell them therefore, **Thus saith Yahuah
Elohyim;** I will make this proverb to cease, and they
shall no more use it as a proverb in Yashar'el; but say
unto them, **The days are at hand, and the effect of every
vision.** For there shall be no more any vain vision nor
flattering divination within the house of Yashar'el. **For
I am Yahuah: I will speak, and the word that I shall
speak shall come to pass;** it shall be no more prolonged:
for in your days, O rebellious house, will I say the word,
and will perform it, saith Yahuah **Elohyim.** Again the
word of Yahuah came to me, saying, Son of man,
behold, they of the house of Yashar'el say, the vision that
he seeth is for many days to come, and he prophesieth of
the times that are far off. Therefore say unto them, **Thus
saith Yahuah Elohyim; <u>There shall none of my words
be prolonged any more, but the word which I have
spoken shall be done, saith Yahuah Elohyim.</u>***
Ezekiel 12:21-28

*As I come to a close with very important book; we must
keep in mind and remember that we are responsible for
speaking, practicing and keeping The Most High
Yahuah's word in our mouth. Then and only then will
we be able by the Ruach of EL; to keep the Pink Tornado
in check.*

Using the Original Names of the Most High!

Scripture Reference:

Proverbs 30:4 Who hath ascended up into heaven, or descended? Who hath gathered the wind in his fists? Who hath bound the waters in a garment? Who hath established all the ends of the earth? **What is HIS NAME, and what is HIS SON'S NAME, if thou canst tell?**

I know most will say; what does it matter?

Rather we use his Hebrew name or not; just as long as I show him respect. Is that RESPECT? Or is it something we picked up and learned from OUR FAMILY, OUR TEACHERS and OUR PREACHERS; if we be truthful with ourselves those aforementioned individuals never thought to look into or research the fact of what the true name of the messiah was.

Throughout the Old Testament the Father's NAME IS NOT MENTIONED AT ALL in THE BIBLE that he wrote and published?

So this is what YOU call RESPECT:

If your name is JOE and I know your name is JOE; I should call you JOE; that's RESPECT! Now you may give me a pass every once in a while to not call you by

your name but to use terms such as my brother, my friend, what's up man, or even in a minor disagreement I may be able to say man or boy please! BUT Respect is when I call you by YOUR APPROPRIATE TITLE and not just calling you some empty vain terminology that IS

WHAT I CALL DISRESPECTFUL!

If you look throughout the Old and New Testament you will see A BLATANT VIOLATION of REPLACING The Most High's name will VAIN and EMPTY words that really hold neither POWER nor any MEANING when in use.

Definition:

Vain: Ineffectual or Unsuccessful; futile: *vain hopes; a vain effort; a vain war.* Without real Significance, Value, or Importance; Baseless or Worthless: *vain pageantry; vain display.* Archaic. Senseless or Foolish.

Exodus 20:7 Thou SHALT NOT TAKE THE NAME of YAHUAH [NOT the LORD] thy ELOHYIM [NOT GOD] IN VAIN; for YAHUAH [NOT the LORD] WILL NOT HOLD HIM GUILTLESS that TAKETH HIS NAME in VAIN:

Oh you thought VAIN was just talking about using a curse word like [for example] [gd] was using The Most High's name in a CURSE WORD but God is not a NAME but A LABEL...If you and I say the word God out loud who are you referring to? **Remember there are others who have god's little [g]** I guess that's supposed to make a difference but who knows RATHER IT'S A CAPITAL LETTER or NOT if you say GOD; I'm I going to ask the question are you capitalizing that G **or** using LOWER case so I'll know who to respond to when you say GOD? No we are not going through all THAT FOOLISHNESS! So by using HIS NAME we can eliminate ALL OF THIS VAIN talk concerning HIS NAME.

The Rabbit hole goes deep! When you see the name of the Most High being eliminated from the holy bible more than Six Thousand Eight Hundred [6800] times; you have to know that this is spiritual warfare at the highest level. The excuse was made that the reason his name was taken out; because it showed him respect. So they called it [The TETRAGAMMATON] [A Revering of The name] saying that it was too holy to proclaim; when in fact the real reason was to hide it from The People of YAHUAH [The Hebrew Israelites] WHO WERE CAPTURED and put in SLAVERY and SCATTERED around the world.

That's why they didn't want us to read because by reading we would have knowledge that it was our ELOHYIM they were talking about…

EXAMPLE:

OLD TESTAMENT: All Capital Letters used…

LORD=Replaced **YAHUAH** (Paleo Hebrew Name)

God=Replaced **ELOHYIM**

NEW TESTAMENT: Capital (L) and Lower Case (ord)…

Lord= Replaced **ADONAI**

Holy Spirit=Replaced **RUACH HaKODESH**

Jesus Christ=YAHUSHA HaMASHIACH

Christian=Netseriy [Nazarene]

Christian=Mashiachiy [Mashiach/Messianic];a follower of YAHUSHA HaMASHIACH

So rather you agree with me or not I must do what I'm compelled and convicted to do; so I can make Abba (Father) happy.

I'm not at all concerned with making you feel comfortable but I am concerned with obeying the master's will.

HERE is FIVE SCRIPTURES REFERENCING HIS NAME:

Psalm 113:1 Praise ye **YAHUAH**. Praise, O servants of **YAHUAH**, praise **THE NAME** of **YAHUAH**.

Psalm 113:2 Blessed be **THE NAME** of **YAHUAH** from this time forth and forevermore.

Psalm 113:3 From the rising of the sun unto the going down of the same **YAHUAH'S NAME** [is] to be praised.

Proverbs 18:10 THE NAME of **YAHUAH** [is] a **STRONG TOWER**: the righteous runneth into **IT** [**HIS NAME**], and is SAFE.

Isaiah 52:6 Therefore **MY PEOPLE shall know MY NAME**: therefore [they shall know] in that day that I [am] HE that doth speak: behold, [it is] i.

James Anthony Durr

Biography

Dr. James A. Durr gave his life to HaMashiach at the age of 20 on 6 January 1984. And at the age of 22 he was called into the ministry. He has help establish ministries in South Korea (1), and Watertown, New York (3). He also served as an Assistant Pastor for four years before he became a pastor. He also served 17 and a half years in the Armed Forces (Army) earning the rank Staff Sergeant (SSG). In 1998 three and a half years (3 ½) before retirement, he was led of Adonai to get out of the military to start a Ministry. Dr. Durr is the Founder of The Word Center International and The Calhoun County College of Theology "A satellite extension of North Carolina College of Theology" in Anniston, Alabama. He has written over 26 books and has been an executive producer and producer on 3 music CD's. He is a highly respected and sought-after preacher. He also holds a Bachelor in Science (BS) in Management of Human Resources, a Masters in Science and Management (MSM), a Masters of Theology in Pastoral Counseling (MPC), a Masters in Theology (MT) and has earned a Doctorate in Theology (Th.D.)

Invitation to HaMashiach

Will you please accept *Yahusha HaMaShiach* into your life today?

The Bible says, "That if thou shalt confess with thy mouth Adonai Yahusha, and shalt believe in thine heart that EL hath raised him from the dead, thou shalt be saved. For with the heart man believeth unto righteousness; and with the mouth confession is made unto salvation. For the scripture saith, Whosoever believeth on him shall not be ashamed." **(Romans 10:9-11).**

Pray this prayer: "Dear Adonai Yahusha, I confess to you that I am a sinner. I believe that you died on the cross and rose from the dead on the third day. I also believe that you shed your precious blood for my sins. I receive your forgiveness and accept you into my heart. I can feel your supernatural love and grace covering me like a blanket. You are my **Redeemer** and **Adonai** of my life. HalleluYAH."

_____Yes, James! I decided to make Adonai Yahusha my Redeemer. Please pray

for me and send me information that can assist me on this journey to heaven.

Name: _____

Address: _____ Zip: _____

Phone:(_____)_____

City: _____ State: _____ Email: _____

To order additional copies contact:

James A. Durr Ministries, Inc.
965 Morton Road
Anniston, Alabama 36205
(256) 282.0313

Email: jamesdurr3@yahoo.com

You can also purchase other powerful books

By: Dr. Durr

Process & Development

$15.00

Taken from the Book of Luke chapter 1 verse 80: This book will explain to you how Elohyim will use four (4) different phases of processing & development; too get us to our divine destiny.

31 Days of Scripture

$8.00

A prescribed book: That will help all of those seeking to memorize a new bible verse each day.

Incredible Dreams

$10.00

The revelation and insight in this book will teach the people of EL why they are not permitted to stop dreaming. It is EL who caused you to dream in the first place.

Divine Breakthrough

(Formally known as Deliverance)

$10.00

This book is designed to show us what's blocking and hindering us from walking in totally victory in HaMashiach.

Poetry in Motion

$8.00

A book of poetry; that minister's to the soul. It is also a book filled with personal sayings that are full of golden wisdom nuggets.

To contact:

Dr. James A. Durr

For A Leadership Seminar, an Evangelistic meeting, or A Conference,

Mail or Call

James Durr Ministries
965 Morton Road
Anniston, Alabama 36205

256.282.0313
Jamesdurr3@yahoo.com

Notes

Notes

Notes

Notes

Notes

Notes

Notes

Notes

Notes

Notes

Notes

Notes

Notes

Notes

Notes

Notes

Notes

Notes

Notes

Notes

Notes

Notes

Notes

Notes

Notes

Notes

Notes

Notes

Notes

Notes

Notes

Notes

Notes

Notes

Notes

Notes

Notes

Notes

Notes

Notes

Notes

Notes

Notes

Notes

Notes

Notes

Notes

Notes

Notes

Notes

Notes

Notes

Notes

Notes

Notes

Notes

Notes

Notes

Notes

Notes

Notes

Notes

Notes

Notes

Notes

Notes

Notes

Notes

Notes

Notes

Notes

Notes

Notes

Notes

Notes

Notes

Notes

Notes

Notes

Reference:

1. The Holy Bible (KJV)
2. Webster's Dictionary
3. **James Strong's:** The New Strong's Exhaustive Concordance of the Bible
4. **My Personal:** Elohyim inspired messages from our Biblical Instructional Training Sessions (B.I.T.S).